AN ACCIDENTAL MASTERPIECE:

POEMS
FROM A COLORFUL LIFE

By Adelia Ritchie, PhD

TABLE OF CONTENTS

ACKNOWLEDGMENTS

Many thanks to the following publications in which these poems appeared:

Cracks in the Plaster — *Leaves of Glass (self-published chapbook)*
Cracks in the Plaster — *Poetry Corners 2018*
They're Just Leaves — *Salish Magazine*
Weeds — *Poetry Corners 2019*
First They'll Come for the Journalists — *What Rough Beast (Indolent Books)*
Indian Pipes — *Salish Magazine*
Tide Pool — *Salish Magazine*

I am thankful to my co-conspirators on Medium.com and Substack.com for individually hosting the bulk of the poems in this volume.

Much love and gratitude to my writing mentor, Nancy Rekow, and to the members of our Tuesday poetry workshop group, where our "poems in the rough" become polished gems. To my poetry pals, Sue Hylen, Dawn Henthorn, Nancy Taylor, and Diane Moser for the years of gentle, caring critiques and "open kimono" poetry. To my journalist friend, Dan Lee, who inspired me to create a fun collection of 75-word novel poems. And to my oldest friend Nancy Walker, who gently informs me that I am not allowed to cry when reading my own poems aloud.

I am especially grateful to that well-known poet who once told me, with a haughty sneer after listening to my open mic readings, that he "doesn't write funny poems."

"Poetry is not the proper antithesis to prose, but to science. Poetry is opposed to science, and prose to metre. The proper and immediate object of science is the acquirement of communication of truth; the proper and immediate object of poetry is the communication of immediate pleasure."

— Samuel T. Coleridge

I. LANDSCAPES

A poem in the night.

Quiet as a late snowfall.

I build a bonfire.

There's an Old Trunk in the Attic

unopened for decades
full of dog show ribbons
desert sage from Sufi camp
worry beads & camping gear
a speckled stone from his farm in France —
locked tight, it keeps its secrets.

She kneels before it
key in hand —
lock rusty, stiff —
gray dust thick with time.
Sensing her presence,
the old trunk shivers.

A lone fly buzzes her ear.
Moisture blooms above her lip,
her cheeks scalding pink.
Sun arrows through the skylight
illuminating snow-clouds of dust,
spiderwebs, half-eaten insects.
Her breath stirs the stillness.

She flips the lock open
and lifts the lid.
Her eyes close —
perfume of sage,
mustiness of aged paper.

Hundreds of thin blue airmail envelopes —
from Frankfurt, Paris, Strasbourg —
his familiar scrawl decorates.
A hot tear drops, sculpting
a tiny crater in the dust.

The ghost of her father
begins to speak.

Dad, on Fire

Four elements — earth, air, fire, water.
Three states — solid, liquid, gas.

"Daddy, what is fire?
If air is gas
and water is liquid
and earth is solid
then, is fire the same as air?"

After a pause he says,
"For children, fire is hot,
dangerous, a thing to avoid.
For a grown-up, fire is comfort, warmth,
security against winter's cold."

"But, Dad, is it a solid, a liquid, or a gas?"

He retorts, "Is it a solid, like a rock?"

"No."

"Is it cool and runny, like water?"

"Um, I guess not."

"Then, what do *you* think it is?"

"But, Dad, if fire is a gas, like air,
why is it orange and blue?"

He considers giving a lesson in quantum physics,
excited electrons, combustion chemistry,
matter, energy, fossil fuels.

He thinks about the Pearl Harbor,
the burning Amazon, natural gas flares,
contrails, climate change.

She watches his face change
with his thoughts.

*"Daddy, it's OK.
Let's do finger paints now!"*

Wine

Fruit of the vine—fine all the time—is wine.

Color my world with reds, whites, rosés

Barbera, Chianti, Toscano, Burgundy

Champagne, Vinho verde, Gewurtz

Pinot Noir from Willamette Valley

Nouveau, oak-barrel aged

Terroir of Central France

Fruit flies drown

Bouquet

Nose

Legs

Taste

Swirl

Taste

Pour

that "La Vielle Ferme" label

for my farmhouse table.

A Crossword Sunday ♡

Sudokus and crosswords
are always a treat

I finished the Times
without having to cheat.

For a lover of words
that's not much of a feat.

It's snowing this Sunday
maybe one or two feet.

The freezer is full
so there's plenty to eat.

Kindling and firewood
will warm my cold feet.

The puzzles are done now
my life is complete.

I Remember Tomorrow

Do you remember next spring
when trees blushed and greened?
And when the drought came next summer?

I remember when fall came before spring
and noon followed midnight,
and the moon waned and then waxed,
or did it wax and then wane?

Is the future
determined by the past?
Or does the future foretell
what happens today?

The laws of physics say
time moves only one way.
But sometimes I recall
next year, next week, next day.

If I walk a circular path
how will I know
if I'm moving forward
or back?

Today I walked the path
that led to yesterday,
where the future bloomed
before my eyes.

Under the Mosquito Net
(near San Isidro de El General, Costa Rica)

a five-inch brown hairy spider
a kissing bug
a young scorpion
a stray ant
a chirping gecko

share my tiny room
on the hill
by the streetlight
above the barking dogs

while motorcycles
scatter wild pebbles
into the dark

I turn out the light
the nightjars serenade
whippoorwill songs
a dog barks
and barks
and barks

I sink into the mattress
cozy in my tropical nest
and drift
and doze
and dream

then bolt upright
at the piercing scream
of a lone mosquito
inside my gossamer tent

she buzzes
and whines
and shrieks
into my ear
lusting for just one taste
one bloodthirsty sip

ZzzzZzzzZzzz
WHAP!

my heart rate slows
night a cool blanket
on my sun-kissed skin

the nightjar sings
the gecko chirps
the jungle sleeps
and so
at last
do I

Apology to My Pet Sitter

—Inspired by Rebecca Foust, "Apology to my OB/Gyn"

Sorry Koukla wouldn't eat
while I was away. I showed you
how to feed her. She takes time,
I said—but you were too impatient.

Sorry she peed on the carpet
when you wouldn't let her out.
She's old and cannot see and
didn't know how to tell you.

Sorry you wouldn't let me
take her to her litter-mate's house.
They love her there and understand.
Sorry I had to leave her with you

but you insisted. She'll be fine
now, she's gaining weight, letting me
brush her mats out, when you wouldn't.
She licked my nose to say she's sorry too.

What to Wear to the Pentagon

Navy whites, Army green,
Air Force blue shade 1620.
Civilian men in midnight blue
starched collars, colorful ties.

I too had a seat at the table
Didn't fetch coffee
Never took notes
Spoke my mind clearly —

and probably too often.
Wore green to Army meetings,
dark blue for Navy
black suit for Air Force.

Sailed on ships in olive drab jumpsuits
in helicopters and jets too
with helmet and boots
red lipstick and mascara

Black leather bomber jacket,
white tee-shirt, black miniskirt,
seamed black stockings when teaching pilots
at the Naval Postgraduate School

Like Kelly McGillis in "Top Gun."
Feeling female and in charge.

But my new suit from Nordstrom's
pale, pastel, and titty pink,

white silk blouse underneath
with sheer hint of cleavage
just out of sight.
Just out of reach.

Please fetch the donuts
bring the coffee
take notes
sit in the back

Don't ask questions
never offer opinions
and 'your facts don't count,
you're just a woman.'

No matter what your rank
you'll get shot down
if you ever wear pink
to the Pentagon.

Sometimes I Wonder

why don't clouds fall from the sky
why are leaves green
what makes the wind blow
why are there rainbows

Sometimes I wish
 I could see through the earth
 breathe underwater
 soar without wings
 walk on the moon

Sometimes I hear
 the sound of falling stardust
 the moon laughing at earth
 mountains breathing
 oceans crying

Sometimes I remember
 hot sand on a tropical beach
 the taste of French butter
 the aroma of Dad's cigar
 the warm scent of you

Sometimes I wonder
 where does the other sock go to hide
 what became of my childhood friend
 where are all those people
 I gave directions to

I Knew the Day Would Come

I knew the day would come
when you
fully realized
that we are soulmates

The way we talk
together
walk together
fit together

We are lock and key
butter and popcorn
potatoes and gravy
scotch and rocks

You come to me
in morning mist
warm and moist
soft and sweet on my skin

I smell you in the wind
earthy, of pine and spruce
of lichens in the understory
of icy mountain springs

I hear your baritone notes
tickling my ears
like butterflies
stopping for nectar

But you're not wild
not free as the breeze

tethered to a mistake
we made a decade ago

You will always be my hero
always in my dreams
alive in my memories

until you're free
to be with me.

Cracks in the Plaster

Classical mustiness
plaster peeling artfully
slightly sagging with time
crumbling here and there

yet fully functional
urban, desired, desirable
beautiful and oft-photographed.

Cities and statues and stucco façades
aging gracefully, remind us
of their long and stellar history.

So sought after, loved,
respected these places.

If only the same were true
for older women's faces.

Where the Wild Goose Goes

Inspired by "Cry of the Wild Goose," Frankie Laine, 1950

From snow-covered tundra
to grassy wetlands
from cloud-capped mountains
to hot desert sands

To stay in one place
to never leave home
a decision we face
to stay or to roam

Roots we put down
reach deeper with time
tie us to ground
forbid us to climb

Like grass to grasslands
cottonwoods to plains
a turtle to wetlands
a fox to its den

With wings one can soar
dive deep into sea
punch holes in the sky
defy gravity

How I've loved your embrace
so familiar your face.
This wandering fool must fly away—
cannot linger another day.

*"You'll see a shadow pass overhead
and find a feather beside the bed."*

They're Just Leaves

A poem in memory of Todd Ramsey, 1950–2021

Lake grass, algae-velveted stones,
floating leaves,
signs of a passing season.
But no one grieves.

They're just leaves.

I hear a sigh,
an autumn cry,
a breath of breeze
stirs the trees,
a cloud scuds by.

My eyes are dry.

All is still.
He had the will,
his to decide
when to cross
to the other side.

My friend just leaves.

Now I can cry.

An Accidental Masterpiece

An artist's poem

Green arm
with red fingers
swims sideways
through crazy-quilt flotsam —
bright swishes of blue
yellow, turquoise, pink

blue fish glide
through pink yellow
blue seaweed
in crowded tide pools

swoops, drips, stabs
stripes, dots, strokes —
a cacophony of colors
accidental

my watercolor
pigment test strip
a masterpiece
of abstraction

II. ON BUFFLEHEAD POND FARM

Nick and Isabel

came to Bufflehead Pond Farm.

My garden watches

In My Garden

Here, in my garden, there's time to recover from daily brain damage and dramas, time to listen to bird songs, time to touch compost-enriched soil that veggies love to sink their feet into, time to feel the cool greenness of my growing leafy children who want nothing more than to end up on my dinner plate.

My dad's old-fashioned French tomatoes — grown on his farm in the Loire Valley — from seeds that were "tiny but oh so powerful," words he once wrote nearly 30 years ago on the inside flap of a tissue-thin blue airmail envelope that held those precious seeds.

Transplants from central France may struggle in our northern dampness, maturing late, striving to ripen their monstrous fruits before the blight takes them down.

I now know that fruiting plants have intelligence — real intelligence — programmed into their DNA over millennia, to ensure the survival of the species even under disastrous circumstances. Diseased, beginning to show rot from the bottom up,

the entire plant becomes self-aware, accepts its impending doom, gathers its remaining energy for one last burst — selects the ripest and healthiest of all its fruits,

channeling everything toward that one fruit, casting off all others, banking everything

on one loaded seed packet to mature and become a lush garden of new baby plants.

As the main stems begin to turn brown, the leaves die, the only remaining green surrounding that one desperate fruit. How can rotted roots and stems provide sustenance to this fruit? How does the plant know what to do? And how does the plant manage to do this?

The baby tomato fruit continues to grow, then begins to fade into yellow,

then orange, and quickly to bright red just as the last gasp of stem support

dies away, and the tomato drops off onto the ground. Alive. Healthy. Full of ripe seeds. Ready to procreate. The supreme sacrifice of the parent for the future of the offspring — the unquenchable drive to produce seed, to create a new generation.

On December 3rd, last year, we dined on the most sumptuous BLT ever created in the known universe, over all time, grown from Dad's magical seeds. They were tiny,

but oh, so powerful.

Sundays

Morning
Sunday sermons confuse me.
Too many questions.
They say,
"Have faith, believe.
Don't think."

I believe in a garden bench
where I can write poems
about freedom from religion
free from Sunday conventions
free from arbitrary rules
free like my seedlings
to grow without twist & warp.

Afternoon

Coffee's cold
crossword finished
comics strewn about—
future shreds for worm compost.

By the duck pond
on my little farm
the veggies cry,
"Pick me! I'm ripe!"
They only wish
to feed my soul.

Evening

Veggies collected,
I thank the earth.
It's Sunday dinner
on the farm.

Autumn

Autumn is upon us now
with fruits of summer stored away.
The sweat that beads upon my brow
rolls down my face this sunny day.

When blight attacks and mold encrusts,
tomatoes rot and squash leaves gray
as bean pods dry in windy gusts,
I thank the earth for her buffet.

Weeds

"How dare you write poems
when I'm full of weeds?"
pouts her neglected garden
beneath an uncertain sky.

Weedy flowers of spring
welcome honeybees
with golden nectar
to feed a growing hive.

Dandelions tunnel
through asphalt;
thistles and shotweeds defy
layers of cedar mulch
to seek sunlight and warmth.

Floaty, feathery seeds cloud the sky,
like tiny umbrellas —
weightless, wild, free —
aloft on a soft breeze.

Future weeds, she thinks,
and only a poet to pull them.

Duck Pond

Springtime at Bufflehead Pond Farm

This duck pond is a weedy mess—
better for birds and bees, I guess.
The Kingfisher's name is Mr. Eddie.
When minnows jump, he's always ready.

The red-winged blackbirds have returned.
For some time I was quite concerned—
their nesting reeds too thinly scattered—
but to them, it scarcely mattered.

A blue heron pair high in the trees
floats down, wings spread, on gentle breeze.
They wait and watch—so calm and still.
To see one strike gives me a thrill!

As evening comes the swallows swarm
in orange and indigo uniform.
Mosquitos never have a chance
when pond birds start their dinner dance.

Out on a Limb-erick

Have you ever seen a Great Blue Heron
look for places to have an affair in?
With legs, neck and wings
stretched out like strings,
he lands in an old tree that's barren.

He flies like a pterodactyl
which females find very attractyl.
He's a lean sex machine,
if you know what I mean,
with his long, sharp-pointed bill.

Watching for neighborhood dogs,
he searches for minnows and frogs.
He postures, he waits,
mainly trolling for dates,
while standing stone still in the bog.

Please watch the Great Blue from a distance.
With lovers he needs no assistance.
He'll jump on and peck 'em
and try not to wreck 'em,
yet finds not one bit of resistance.

The moral of this story I've forgotten,
my old brain resembling soft cotton.
But when wild birds in a tree
start making whoopee,

just trust that they're both besotten.

III. POEM NOVELS IN 75 WORDS

Just a meteor?
I want to believe I saw
a true UFO

The Language Barrier

It was a dark and stormy night
on their return from post-war Japan.
Just three years old,
she wanted to make a very good impression
on her Most Honorable Southern Ancestor,
invoking her deepest bow.

"Takasan ami neh?" she said
in poor imitation of her Japanese tutors.
"Much rain, yes?"
Her parents beamed with pride
at their precocious daughter.

"How dare you allow
my only great-grandchild
to associate with those barbarians!"
her great-grandmother spat.

The Old Trunk

There's an old trunk in the attic,
filled with letters from Dad,
written from Paris, Frankfurt,
Hügelsheim, Montrésor, exotic places.

Should I open it? I wondered,
or should I be content with memories,
however altered by time they may be.

"There's a poem to be written,"
said my writing mentor.
Will it be a poem,
or will it be a tragedy,
without suspense, without humor?

Opening it, I could sense his presence…
and his resurrection.

After the Hunt

Perched high in the ancient weeping willow tree,
she waited for the hunters to return,
drooling in anticipation
of her father's spicy recipes
for pheasant and venison.

The screened porch
on the shady side of the house
filled with the tangy scents
of blood, guts and feathers.

She wondered why she was forbidden
to open the mysterious door at the back of the porch
that led to the spidery basement
where the wine was kept.

Anti-gravity

Until now she hadn't understood
that gravity didn't affect her.
Waking with a start,
she found herself
in the corner of her room,
caught in an eddy
near the ceiling.

Her mother had always
called her an airhead.
In school, her classmates
called her a lightweight.
She had assumed it was
because she wasn't pudgy
and bosomy like the other girls.

Leaving no footprints
she sneaked up on her mother
and cut the apron strings.

The French Lesson

One taste of that frothy cappuccino
at Maxim's that April afternoon
changed her life.

Her father had taken her there
to teach her how to flirt properly.

"The very next woman that passes us by
will fall in love with me," he predicted.
"Observez-moi, ma petite."

Their eyes met, he smiled.
The old woman flushed, straightened, smiled shyly,
touched her hair, and moved past us with grace.

"So, my dear, now it's your turn."

Last Night in Florence

It was their last night in Florence.
Restaurant reservations were made and confirmed.
Their special outfits for celebrating
their last meal (*la ultima cena*) in Italy
were hanging in their closets, eager to be shown off.

"Ciao! Bella!" Bruno greeted the four women
as he always greeted women,
with multiple ass fondles.

"Tonight we have the most special porcherino
made from boar's milk.
It takes great skill when milking a boar
to avoid its Tuscans."

The Little Man in Her Head

Perched on his tiny shelf
at the back of her brain,
the little man who
gave her a report each morning
knew she was onto him.

They had often come to blows
back when she was trying
to quit smoking,
but this time it was different.

Once she realized she could
think for herself,
his desperate plea —
"If you leave me, I'm going with you" —
no longer worked.

Determined, her neurosurgeon began the extraction.

Late Night Cuppa

In over 20 years of serving burnt coffee
to late-night drunks, she had never felt
such a body-slam to her amygdala,
having felt only numbness for too long.

His musky scent invaded her nostrils and lungs,
metastasizing through her like earthworms
sliding through rich damp soil.
His look told her everything she needed to know.

Her steady hand moved toward him.
Heaving a sigh, she poured him another cup.

Scotch on the Docks

Damn. The tissue box is empty again,
she whined, reaching instead for her Scotch.
Arianna had always preferred spiced rum
until she met Rafael,
the tall stranger standing on the dock,
alone, in the rain.

Like the condensation on her icy glass,
tears flowed down her cheeks.
Watching Rafael sail away,
she felt as empty as that tissue box.
She turned back to her Scotch.

"Hello, do you need a hanky?"
offered the handsome stranger.

Inshallah

There could be
no surprises left,
she thought,
as she made her way
through the ancient market,
wielding her cane
like a scimitar
against the small brown gypsy boys
begging for *just one Dirham, inshallah.*

Pungent scents of paprika, chilies,
garlic, camel dung, smoky incense
invaded her nostrils
as mosquitos helicoptered
down inside her veil
to drink from descending
rivulets of sweat.

At last, desperately thirsty,
she spotted *Rick's Café Americain*,
certain he would be there.

Hot Pursuit

Blue and white striped awnings
made fluffing noises in the breeze.
Calm waters reflected the night sky
like a torch singer's sequined gown.

She was determined,
on her last night in Cannes,
to capture his attention.

She wanted the man with the red cravat
and gold-capped cane,
the man of many rumors,
the man who would not be had.
She wanted him so bad.

"Hands behind your head and spread 'em!"
she commanded.

Arachnophilia

Exhausted from the long trip,
she unpacked,
putting things away
in her tiny room
above the studio workshop.

No air conditioning needed
at 3700 feet altitude.
There were a few ants
around the sink drain,
nothing to worry about,
and the mosquito net above her cozy bed
had just a few holes.

Under the sink,
her 8-inch brown tarantula roommate slept,
not minding the sudden intrusion of light
as the cupboard door opened.

Fatal Attraction?

Desperately attracted
to dangerous men,
the witch knew what was at stake—
hopefully not herself.

Like a stalking cat in high grass
she approached,
cape billowing in the wind.

She felt that familiar twat-twinkle
signal of imminent danger,
but she could not turn back now.
She cast her spell on the dark stranger.

Should've known his teeth were razor-sharp
to puncture painlessly — anesthetizing her.
Would she survive?
How would she know?

Kicking the Habit

The nun ducked into a confession booth
and moments later reemerged
in a red dress and high heels.

"How can God allow cancer", she wondered
Storms, drought, failed crops,
floods, disease, and wars
should have not been allowed
by an all-powerful, beneficent god.

Her faith in such a deity
could no longer withstand the reality
of wars and other deadly disasters.

She told the priest,
"I'm no longer in the habit
of practicing religion."

Rrrrrromance

She could tell by his random stacking
of sticks and uncut rounds
he knew little about building a wood fire.
Raised in the country
alongside an intelligent pig,
she wondered if his city ways
would divide them.

Her eyes, large and brown,
her hair long and fluffy —
his, shaggy, whitish, shedding
on the navy blue chair
next to the fireplace.

She approached on all fours,
submissive, murmuring softly.

"Rrrrrrr…," he growled, invitingly.

Tides of Change

Blowing sandy bubbles in anticipation,
sand dollars, baby crabs and anemones
knew the tide was coming.

But in her quest for the perfect moon shell,
she was oblivious
to the cries of cormorants and sea gulls above her.

Seaweed fanned out
like a starlet's hair on the casting couch pillow
and clams slammed shut against the incoming waves.

Homeless and vulnerable,
the panicked hermit crab
found her perfect new home —
a blue plastic tampon case.

As the Worm Turns

"What is that skin-desiccating orb in the sky?"
she wondered, having endured months
of unending gloom.

Her life had been a good one,
if not luxurious, and she never went without
the plentiful food that appeared
in the compost bin almost daily.
Her dark subterranean abode was warm
and filled with contented offspring.

This day, though, as she writhed in warm sunshine
unable to get her bearings,
she knew was to be her last.

The Plot Sickens

Under the blazing sun,
beans, cukes, taters, 'maters,
peas, and carrots
vined, twined and marched upward,
joining the hops and artichokes
to strategize the farm takeover.

"It's a plot," she thought.
"No, it's about 42 plots, you idiot,"
the veggies shouted.

Grapevines strangled her,
raspberries mauled,
pumpkins snaked,
cucumbers snagged her ankles
as she dragged the garden hose to bring them water.

"We've bean had,
and you don't carrot all about us.
Lettuce outta here!"

IV. PLANET HOME

Jungle denizens

petri dish for pathogens

It's so warm today

The climate heats up

new virus — can we adapt?

herd immunity

Indian Pipes

—also known as the Ghost Plant

"Stop," I said. "Indian Pipes."
Ghostly white,
tiny vampires reaching up
from moist loam
beneath an ancient forest.

You picked a few,
a colorless bouquet
wilting in your hand
without its fungal web
to nourish it.

"Let the ghosts sleep,"
I said, "and hug the trees
that feed them."

Tide Pool

Wet warm sand squishes
    between my naked toes
the foamy edge of a tiny wave
    slides across my foot
        erasing its sand mud crust

my foot seeks soft places
    away from fragile sea life
hiding in gnarled nooks
    under rocks
        inside abandoned shells

a clam filter feeds
    as I approach
slamming shut
    to protect
        its tender soft parts

a tiny crab skitters
    tickles my toes
a ring of anemones
    decorates the sand
        drawing circles with their offspring

baby crabs hide in seaweed knots
    a sand dollar nursery
a galaxy of sea stars
    paint their presence orange and purple
        on the sandy bottom

the tide slides closer
        submerging life forms
shooing human toes away
        from tomorrow's sunken treasures

Where the Woods Were

An ode to a lost forest

Where the woods were
a trillium bloomed
in the shade
of an ancient
cedar tree

snowberries peeked
through branches
stealing sunlight
from mosses

sword ferns unfurled
green wings
fanned out
from hairy backbones

tiny shrew families
dug earthworms
woodpeckers
and wood ducks
made nests
in knotholes

salamanders slithered
where deer hooves trod
raccoons played
and cougars roared

where the woods were.

I Dream of Summer

Brazen bluebirds
in red maple trees
a goldfinch pair
high in a Douglas fir
redwing blackbirds
nesting in verdant pond reeds

flowers on the wing
feathered bouquets
chirp, whistle, trill
in technicolor notes
a symphony of hues
a rainbow of tunes

A cat, an eagle,
a coyote, my dog,
a delight of ducks
geese and cormorants
a great blue heron
a chattering kingfisher
a red-tailed hawk

A glass of wine
an easy chair
a dock on the pond
and pine-scented air

Forest Tree

My family studies
records of our ancestors'
births, deaths, offspring
branches reaching
deep into the past
into Scotland
England
France—
          our family tree.

I practice art,
paintings in pastels,
acrylics, watercolors,
multimedia sometimes.
Flowers and landscapes
sun and rain
summer and fall
gnarly trunks and bent branches—
          my artist tree.

I ponder the dance
of atoms, molecules,
electrons, their mystery
within the old oak
that leans protectively
over my studio
making energy inside
its leaves. The sun warms
and catalyzes, brings life
          to my chemist tree.

This ancient tree
shelters songbirds,
tree frogs, ants and weevils,
webbed in fungal communication
with the forest, the grass—
with me.
Its sweet oxygen breath
intoxicates, calms, inspires—
          my poet tree.

Apocalypse Now

When the storms came
and the winds blew
and the roofs flew
and the trees snapped
and the flags flapped
and the waves broke
and the houses fell
and the mudslides
brought down hillsides
then the sun shone
and the ground baked
and the trees dried
and the fires burned
filled the dead air
with dust and smoke
then the birds choked
and the squirrels croaked
and the worms fried
and the earth died.

Water

what the next wars will be about

damp moist dewy wet
humid steaming sticky sweat
rain hail sleet snow
fog mist cloud rainbow

brook river creek stream
pond lake ocean sea
raft boat surfboard ski
thunderstorm waterspout tsunami

cyclone typhoon hurricane
wild northeaster wind-wave train
ice liquid vapor slush
flow drip burble gush

torrent rapids waterfall
glacier iceberg plump snowball
drink bathe swim splash shower
sprinkle it on a bright red flower.

V. MÉMOIRE À VILLANELLES
(Memoir in Villanelles)

Chromosomes unzip

rings of genes, one side, one edge

a Möbius trip

One Hell of a Villanelle

A villanelle about writing a villanelle

The first time you write a villanelle,
you'll master the form — but not outright —
it's a poetry form that's straight out of hell.

Do it just once, and then say farewell!
Accept the challenge, get over your fright
the first time you write a villanelle.

Your rhythms are awkward, rhymes just won't gel!
You'll ponder all evening, stay up all night,
it's a poetry form that's straight out of hell.

There's no excuse if you feel unwell.
Just finish the job and you'll be alright
the first time you write a villanelle.

Your writing goes smoother with good zinfandel.
You're getting the rhymes down, keeping it tight.
It's a poetry form that's straight out of hell.

Don't give up yet! You're doing so well!
You'll use all your paper and all your graphite
the first time you write a villanelle,
this poetry form that's straight out of hell.

The Ten Dollar Dress

A teen-aged girl in deep distress
had lost her faith in brotherly love
and left that town in a ten-dollar dress.

What sin is love? Did she transgress?
Their judgment was unworthy of
a sweet young girl in deep distress.

Obedience, deference, godliness —
false piety she was so tired of.
She left that town in a ten-dollar dress.

"We know what you've done! You must confess!"
Why do they curse? How dare they shove
an innocent girl in deep distress!

She'd escape to a place no one could guess —
her life, her roots, she'd let go of
and leave that town in a ten-dollar dress.

From across the room his eyes caress.
This handsome Frenchman's worthy of
this lovelorn girl in deep distress
who came to town in a ten-dollar dress.

Dancin' at the Whiskey A-Go-Go

In the good old days, a long time ago
she was young and hot, a good lookin 'blonde
who loved to dance at the Whiskey-A-Go-Go

She danced the Boogaloo and the Mashed Potato
in the white go-go boots that she had donned,
in the good old days, a long time ago

High up in her bird cage, she put on her show
flirting with the boys, winking her *"C'mon!"*
when she was dancin 'at the Whiskey-A-Go-Go

Her love of dance she'd never outgrow.
She longed to study at La Sorbonne
in the good old days, a long time ago

But tonight she looked down at the scene below,
and thought, "Who will die next in Vietnam
while I'm dancin 'at the Whiskey-A-Go-Go?"

"What's wrong with this world, I want to know!"
She thought of her lover, shot dead by Viet Cong
in the good old days, a long time ago
while she was dancin 'at the Whiskey-A-Go-Go.

First They'll Come for the Journalists

First they'll come for the journalists.
They'll toss them in jail like murder suspects,
but those lying meddlers won't be missed.

Writers, reporters and cartoonists —
then atheists, leftists, and network execs —
but first they'll come for the journalists.

Science and data, officials insist,
have no bearing on climate effects.
Those lying reporters won't be missed.

Physicians, teachers and scientists,
their threat to this government is more complex,
but first they'll come for the journalists.

If the media's lying, does truth exist?
They'll get 'em for treason or other pretext.
Those fact-checking meddlers won't be missed.

Now handcuffed and gagged, they no longer resist
And we don't know what happened next.
First they came for the journalists
Those lying meddlers won't be missed.

She Wasn't Young

She wasn't young, she knew the score.
She'd like, she'd lust, she'd feel the heat
but she'd never been in love before.

The men she'd known were just a bore —
her last was puffed up with conceit.
She wasn't young, she knew the score.

To men she'd say, "Mmmm, je t'adore."
She'd entertained the Royal Fleet!
But she'd never been in love before.

She'd tried them all, let them explore,
checked out each man's balance sheet.
She wasn't young, she knew the score.

Her looks attracted men galore —
she'd tossed them out like rotten meat —
'cause she'd never been in love before.

But when that man came through her door
she knew he'd make her life complete.
She wasn't young, she knew the score,
and she'd never been in love before.

Illicit Love

It's time to go, the hour is near.
I love you, girl, you're my best friend,
but she must never find you here.

We've known each other many a year,
through ups and downs and 'round the bend.
Now it's time to go, the hour is near.

We're a perfect fit, that much is clear.
It's difficult to comprehend,
but she must never find you here.

I pace the floor 'til you appear,
and wish our time we could extend
but it's time to go, the hour is near.

You know that I am quite sincere —
the two of us a perfect blend —
but she must never find you here.

Our love is true, you mustn't fear,
but I'm not free, I can't pretend.
It's time to go, the hour is near.
She must never find you here.

Garden Villanelle

Summer is approaching fast.
I'll grow some squash, I'll grow some beans
I'll do my best to make them last.

I'm down each spring and feel harassed
when it rains and sleets, weather intervenes
but summer is approaching fast.

I worked each day in summers past,
on Sundays toiled in Holy jeans!
I've done my best to make them last.

Reds and greens in high contrast,
our salads have the greenest greens
and summer is approaching fast.

My garden's bounty's unsurpassed.
Hand-sow, hand-pick, use no machines.
I do my best to make it last.

With healthful food for my repast
I gobble up superb cuisines.
Summer is approaching fast.
I'll do my best to make it last.

We've Stowed the Plow

Cool weather is upon us now.
The beans are shelled, the corn is sweet.
Summer's done, we've stowed the plow.

Towering sunflowers take a bow—
Plenty of seeds for chicks to eat.
Fall weather is upon us now.

Herbs are dried, hay for the cow,
potatoes stored, dug the last beet.
Summer's done, we've stowed the plow.

"Please stack the wood," yelled the hausfrau.
"When snowfall comes, we'll need the heat!"
'Cause winter is a'coming now.

Warm woolens cover toe to brow,
my cut-off shorts now obsolete.
Summer's done, we've stowed the plow.

I'd sell my soul to disallow
this change of seasons to repeat.
But winter is upon us now.
Summer's done, we've stowed the plow.

· · ·

ABOUT THE AUTHOR

A long-time resident of the great Pacific Northwest, and currently a resident of San Isidro de El General, Costa Rica, Adelia Ritchie is a serial entrepreneur, scientist, educator, artist, and writer. Her articles and papers have been featured in a wide variety of publications, from science journals to pet product magazines, and is a contributing editor at Salish Magazine. She has consulted worldwide on topics of systems engineering and climate change issues.